THE WOMAN OF ENNEAGRAM 9

LOVE, MARRIAGE AND SUCCESS EDITION

FREE GIFT

Get a FREE book on the Enneagram & Female Sexuality! Discover:
Fears & desires
Sexual traits
Sexual compatibility
Tips for a fulfilling sex life
Limited time offer!

The woman of Enneagram 9: Love marriage success edition

Enneagram For Women, Volume 9

Maria Rondon

Published by Maria Rondon, 2024.

THE WOMAN OF ENNEAGRAM 9: LOVE MARRIAGE SUCCESS EDITION

First edition. March 28, 2024.

Written by Maria Rondon.

<u>OR CLICK HERE</u>[1]

---

1. https://divinemessenger.site/free-gift/

ENNEAGRAM 9 FOR WOMEN.

Library of Congress Cataloging-in-Publication Data:
Rondon, Maria.
Enneagram 9 for women / Maria Rondon. — 1st ed.

CONTENT

Chapter 1: Charting Your Course: The Enneagram and the Peaceful Woman

Introduction to the Enneagram
    The Enneagram for Peacemakers:

Chapter 2: The Peaceful Woman: Embracing Your Desire for Harmony

Core Motivations & Fears:

Instinctual Subtypes:

Chapter 3: Finding Your Voice: The Enneagram and Authentic Expression

Challenges with Self-Assertion:

Strategies for Healthy Expression:

Chapter 4: Beyond Merging: Relationships and Preserving Identity

Merging Patterns: how Type 9s lose themselves in relationships to gain peace.

Healthy Boundaries: maintaining a sense of self while fostering fulfilling relationships.

Chapter 5: Presence and Stillness: Finding Your Calm

Tapping into Inner Peace: the Type 9 woman's natural reservoir of calmness.

Mindfulness Techniques: meditations and practices to enhance inner peace and presence.

Chapter 6: Conquering Inertia: Motivation and Taking Action

Understanding Apathy: how the Type 9's desire for peace can sometimes lead to procrastination and passivity.

Strategies for Motivation: practical tools for setting goals and initiating action.

Chapter 7: Awakening Your Energy: Movement and Reconnection

Movement as Medicine: how exercise and embodied practices can counter Type 9 inertia and foster vibrancy.

Finding Joy in Movement: movement forms enjoyable for Type 9s, focusing on connection, not force.

Chapter 8: Self-Care for the Peacemaker: Rest and Restoration

Combating Self-Neglect: the Type 9's tendency to prioritize everyone else's needs before their own.

Restorative Practices: self-care techniques that restore energy and nurture inner peace, emphasizing the importance of rest for Type 9s.

Creating a Nourishing Environment: how to create a peaceful and supportive home space conducive to relaxation for the Type 9 woman.

Chapter 9: Handling Anger: Healthy Expression for the Peacemaker

Hidden Anger: how Type 9s suppress or minimize their anger to maintain peace.

Identifying Anger Triggers: identify situations and behaviors that spark their suppressed anger.

Strategies for Expressing Anger: constructive ways to express anger without compromising their peacemaking instincts.

Chapter 10: Unveiling Your Wings: Exploring the Nuances of Your Personality

Understanding Wings: how Type 9w8 (more assertive) and Type 9w1 (more introspective) influence personality.

Strengths and Challenges: the gifts and struggles unique to each wing combination for Type 9 women.

Chapter 11: Growth and Transformation: Integration and Disintegration

Path of Integration (to Type 3): how Type 9s can embody healthy Type 3 traits like action and goal orientation.

Path of Disintegration (to Type 6): how Type 9s under stress may exhibit Type 6 anxieties and self-doubt.

The Goal of Growth: healthy integration, strategies to manage disintegration.

Chapter 12: Workbook

Chapter 1

Charting Your Course: The Enneagram and the Peaceful Woman

Introduction to the Enneagram:

The Enneagram, an intricate and ancient system of personality understanding, offers profound insights into the human psyche, illuminating the diverse pathways through which individuals navigate the world. Among its nine distinct types, the journey of the Type 9 woman stands out for its emphasis on peace, harmony, and the often subconscious desire to merge with the wills and identities of others. This chapter aims to delve into the realms most pertinent to the Type 9 women, exploring their aversion to conflict, their quest for harmony, and their tendency to merge with their surroundings, all through the lens of the Enneagram's rich historical and philosophical backdrop.

Type 9 women are the quintessential embodiment of seeking peace and harmony, not merely as external conditions but as internal states of being. This pursuit is deeply rooted in the Enneagram's historical evolution, which underscores the significance of understanding oneself to navigate life's tumultuous seas with grace. The Enneagram's journey from ancient wisdom to modern psychological tool reflects a timeless quest for knowledge, self-awareness, and, ultimately, inner peace. For Type 9 women, this quest is not only a personal endeavor but a universal one, echoing the Enneagram's own storied history.

The aversion to conflict in Type 9 women can be likened to the Enneagram's subtle emergence from obscurity into the consciousness of the Western world. Just as the Enneagram was not initially understood or widely accepted, Type 9 women often find themselves retreating from conflict, preferring to remain in the background rather than disturb the equilibrium. Their peace-seeking nature is a testament to the Enneagram's overarching philosophy that harmony within the self leads to harmony with the universe. Type 9 women embody this philosophy, striving to maintain a serene and untroubled existence, even if it means sacrificing their own desires or voices in the process.

Harmony-seeking, another hallmark of the Type 9 personality, reflects the Enneagram's integration of diverse spiritual and philosophical traditions. Just as the Enneagram synthesizes these varied perspectives into a coherent system, Type 9 women seek to bring together disparate elements in their environments, striving for a unity that resonates with the Enneagram's core principle of interconnectedness. Their natural inclination towards consensus and accommodation mirrors the Enneagram's own conciliatory essence, revealing a deep-seated belief in the possibility of universal harmony.

The tendency of Type 9 women to merge with others is perhaps the most poignant reflection of the Enneagram's purpose: to transcend the ego and realize a deeper connection with the self and, by extension, with others. This merging is not merely a loss of identity but a profound act of empathy and understanding, mirroring the Enneagram's aim to bridge the gaps between disparate personality types. For Type 9 women, merging with others is both a challenge and a gift, offering a unique opportunity to experience the world from multiple perspectives, even if it means occasionally losing sight of their own.

In exploring the Enneagram's relevance to Type 9 women, we are reminded of the system's enduring wisdom and its capacity to guide individuals towards a deeper understanding of themselves and their place in the world. The journey of the Type 9 woman, marked by a desire for peace, harmony, and unity, is a testament to the Enneagram's timeless appeal and its profound ability to illuminate the complexities of the human spirit. As we chart the course of the peaceful woman through the Enneagram, we uncover not only the nuances of Type 9 but the essence of the Enneagram itself: a tool for self-discovery, personal growth, and, ultimately, for finding one's way back to the tranquil waters of inner peace

The Enneagram for Peacemakers: Unveiling the Path to Voice and Needs for Type 9 Women

The Enneagram, an age-old and profound framework for understanding human personality, offers a unique perspective on the journey towards self-knowledge and growth. It serves as a compass for individuals navigating the complex seas of identity, motivation, and interpersonal relationships. Among its nine types, the Type 9, or the Peacemaker, embodies the quest for internal and external peace, often at the cost of their own voice and needs. This chapter delves into how the Enneagram, with its rich historical tapestry and philosophical depth, can empower Type 9 women to find their voice and assert their needs, thus charting a course toward a more balanced and fulfilling existence.

Rooted in ancient wisdom, the Enneagram's origins weave through the tapestry of human history, drawing on spiritual and philosophical traditions that span the globe. Its development, particularly in the 20th century, marked a pivotal turn in understanding the dynamics of human personality. For Type 9 women, the Enneagram offers a mirror to their soul, reflecting the serene waters of their inner peace, alongside the undercurrents of unexpressed desires and silenced voices. The historical journey of the Enneagram itself, from esoteric origins to modern psychological tool, mirrors the journey Type 9s must undertake—from the quiet shores of peacekeeping to the bold act of asserting one's true self.

The teachings of George Gurdjieff, Peter Ouspensky, and subsequent scholars illuminate the path for Type 9s. Gurdjieff's travels and teachings highlighted the importance of awakening to one's true self, a message that resonates deeply with Type 9 women. These teachings encourage Type 9s to explore beyond their comfort zones of agreement and accommodation, guiding them toward a deeper understanding of their intrinsic worth and the importance of their needs and desires.

For Type 9 women, the Enneagram does not merely categorize them as peacekeepers but delves deeper into the essence of what it means to seek peace. It recognizes their natural inclination to harmonize with their environment, to listen, and to empathize. Yet, it also challenges them to consider the cost of peace at the expense of self. The teachings of the Enneagram encourage Type 9s to confront their inner fears—fear of conflict, fear of disconnection, fear of their own power—and to recognize these fears as signposts on the journey toward self-realization.

The Enneagram offers Type 9s practical tools and practices to find their voice and assert their needs. Through self-reflection, meditation, and the Enneagram's rich body of knowledge, Type 9 women can begin to articulate their desires, set boundaries, and engage in conflict with grace and courage. This process of self-discovery and assertion is not a departure from their nature but an evolution towards a more authentic and empowered self.

Furthermore, the Enneagram's holistic view of personality encourages Type 9 women to integrate their peacekeeping qualities with assertiveness and directness. It reveals that true peace is not the absence of conflict but the presence of authenticity and integrity. By embracing their Enneagram type, Type 9s learn that their voice and needs are not only valid but essential for creating genuine harmony in their relationships and their inner world.

the Enneagram serves as a guiding light for Type 9 women, illuminating the path from self-effacement to self-assertion. Through the wisdom of this ancient system, Type 9s can navigate the journey of finding their voice and asserting their needs with confidence and clarity. The historical and philosophical richness of the Enneagram provides not just a backdrop but a foundation for this transformative journey. As Type 9 women embrace the teachings of the Enneagram, they chart a course not only towards personal growth but towards a more profound and resonant peace—the peace that comes from knowing and expressing one's true self.

Chapter 2:

The Peaceful Woman: Embracing Your Desire for Harmony

Core Motivations & Fears: Delving into the Type 9's Yearning for Inner Peace, Dread of Conflict, and the Quest for Harmony

At the heart of the Enneagram Type 9 woman lies a profound longing for peace and harmony, not just as an external condition but as a deep-seated inner need. This chapter explores the intricate web of motivations and fears that drive the Type 9 woman, guiding her actions and shaping her interactions with the world. It delves into her quest for inner tranquility, her aversion to conflict, and her continual striving for a harmonious existence, all through the enriching perspective of the Enneagram's storied journey.

The core motivation of the Type 9 woman is her pursuit of peace. This is not merely the absence of discord but a profound state of equilibrium and contentment within herself and in her surroundings. This desire is rooted in the belief that peace is the ultimate harbinger of happiness and stability. Like the ancient Pythagoreans and Neoplatonists, who saw harmony as a fundamental principle of the universe, the Type 9 woman seeks to embody this principle in her life, using it as a compass to navigate the complexities of human relationships and the self.

However, this longing for peace is twinned with a deep-seated fear of conflict, which Type 9s perceive as a threat to their inner and outer world's stability. They dread disturbances in their environment, not because they lack the courage to face them, but because they value the collective well-being over individual confrontation. This aversion can lead them to suppress their own needs and desires, choosing instead to merge with the preferences and wills of others to maintain harmony. It is a testament to their selfless nature but also highlights their struggle to assert their individuality.

The need for harmony in Type 9 women extends beyond mere conflict avoidance; it is a genuine desire to see the world as a cohesive whole, where differences are not just tolerated but embraced. They are the quintessential mediators, endowed with the unique ability to understand and empathize with diverse perspectives. This ability is a reflection of the Enneagram's own history, a system that integrates various spiritual and philosophical traditions into a unified understanding of human nature. Type 9s embody the Enneagram's spirit, seeking to bridge gaps and create unity in diversity.

Yet, the journey of the Type 9 woman is not without its challenges. Her quest for peace can sometimes lead to complacency, where the fear of upsetting the status quo results in a life unexamined and potentials unrealized. The Enneagram, with its rich tapestry of insights and practices, offers Type 9 women a path to overcoming these obstacles. By engaging with the Enneagram's teachings, they can learn to balance their peace-seeking nature with the courage to confront and express their true selves.

The teachings of Gurdjieff, Ouspensky, Naranjo, and others in the Enneagram tradition encourage Type 9 women to awaken to their own worth, to recognize the beauty in their desire for peace, and to confront their fears of conflict with wisdom and grace. These teachings provide them with the tools to navigate their inner world, to assert their needs and desires, and to fulfill their quest for harmony without losing sight of themselves.

In embracing their core motivations and confronting their fears, Type 9 women embark on a transformative journey. It is a journey that leads them to discover the strength within their gentleness, the assertiveness within their peacefulness, and the profound sense of self that emerges when they truly engage with their desire for harmony. The Enneagram, with its ancient roots and its embrace of diverse traditions, serves as a guide for Type 9 women, helping them to chart a course towards a more balanced, harmonious, and fulfilling life.

Instinctual Subtypes: Unraveling the Nuances of a Type 9 Woman's Personality

The Enneagram, with its roots entwined in the ancient soil of spiritual and philosophical wisdom, offers a lens through which to view the multifaceted nature of the human psyche. For the Type 9 woman, known for her peaceful demeanor and harmonious essence, the concept of instinctual subtypes adds layers of depth and nuance to her personality. These subtypes—self-preservation, social, and sexual (also known as one-to-one)—serve as the undercurrents that influence her motivations, fears, and behaviors, shaping the unique expression of her quest for peace and harmony.

Self-Preservation Type 9: The Comfort Seeker

The self-preservation Type 9 woman embodies the desire for peace through comfort and stability in her physical environment. This subtype is driven by an instinctual need to maintain personal safety and ensure that basic life necessities are met. The self-preservation Type 9 seeks harmony by creating a serene and comfortable living space, avoiding any form of physical discomfort or upheaval that could disturb her inner tranquility. Like the ancient teachings that emphasize the balance of the physical and spiritual realms, the self-preservation Type 9 strives to align her surroundings with her inner state of peace, making her home a sanctuary from the chaos of the outside world.

Social Type 9: The Community Peacemaker

The social Type 9 woman finds her path to peace through her relationships and the community. This subtype is motivated by the need to belong and to contribute to the greater good, often putting the needs of the group above her own. The social Type 9 works tirelessly to ensure harmony within her community, mediating conflicts and bringing people together. Her peace-seeking nature is outwardly focused, driven by a vision of a united world where everyone feels accepted and understood. This mirrors the Enneagram's historical role in bridging diverse spiritual and philosophical traditions, as the social Type 9 seeks to create a bridge between individuals, fostering a sense of collective harmony and understanding.

Sexual Type 9: The Intimate Harmonizer

The sexual, Type 9 woman channels her desire for peace into her close relationships, seeking deep and harmonious connections with others. This subtype is driven by an instinctual need for intimacy, where peace is found in the understanding and merging with another. The sexual Type 9 is passionate about her partnerships, investing deeply in the emotional and physical closeness that comes with true connection. Her approach to achieving harmony is personal and direct, engaging in relationships with a depth that seeks to dissolve the boundaries between self and other. This reflects the Enneagram's esoteric origins, where unity and oneness with the cosmos were central themes, as the sexual Type 9 strives for a profound union with her loved ones.

The understanding of these instinctual subtypes enriches our comprehension of the Type 9 woman, revealing the diverse ways in which her core motivations and fears manifest. Whether she seeks peace through personal comfort, community harmony, or intimate connections, the subtype distinctions provide a framework for the Type 9 woman to navigate her journey towards self-awareness and growth. In embracing her instinctual subtype, the Type 9 woman gains insights into her unique path to achieving inner peace and harmony, further illuminating the intricate dance between her desires, fears, and the universal quest for tranquility that defines her essence. Through the lens of the Enneagram and its profound historical and philosophical roots, the Type 9 woman finds not only a map to her own soul but also a guide to living in harmony with the world around her.

Chapter 3:

Finding Your Voice: The Enneagram and Authentic Expression

Challenges with Self-Assertion: Navigating Type 9's Hesitance in Expressing Needs and Setting Boundaries

In the rich tapestry of the Enneagram's wisdom, Type 9s embody a unique paradox: they possess a deep reservoir of empathy and understanding, yet often struggle to voice their own needs and desires. This chapter delves into the heart of the Type 9's journey towards authentic expression, exploring the challenges they face in self-assertion and the tendency to prioritize harmony over personal boundaries. Drawing from the Enneagram's storied past and its philosophical underpinnings, we uncover insights into the Type 9's path towards finding their voice amidst the silence of acquiescence.

Type 9s, known for their peacekeeping nature, navigate life with a gentle steadiness, seeking to maintain balance and avoid conflict. This inclination, while fostering an environment of tranquility, often comes at the expense of their own voice. The historical evolution of the Enneagram, from ancient spiritual roots to a modern tool for self-discovery, mirrors the Type 9's own journey of unfolding. Just as the Enneagram was embraced by early thinkers like Gurdjieff and Ouspensky, who recognized its potential to bridge the gap between inner knowledge and outer expression, Type 9s too are on a quest to bridge their inner world of desires with their outward expression.

The challenge for Type 9s lies in their deep-rooted aversion to conflict and disruption. Their inherent belief in the value of peace and harmony often leads them to suppress their desires, needs, and, subsequently, their boundaries. This tendency not only dims their voice but can also lead to a sense of inner fragmentation, where their true self becomes obscured by the amalgamation of others' needs and expectations. The writings of the ancient Pythagoreans and Neoplatonists, with their emphasis on harmony and the alignment of the soul with universal truths, echo the Type 9's internal struggle between the desire for peace and the need for authentic self-expression.

To navigate these challenges, Type 9s must embark on a journey of self-discovery, much like the spiritual seekers and philosophers who contributed to the Enneagram's development. This journey involves recognizing and valuing their own worth, understanding that their needs and desires are as valid as those of the people around them. By confronting their fear of conflict and disruption, Type 9s can begin to see that asserting themselves does not necessarily lead to disharmony but can instead foster deeper, more authentic relationships.

Setting boundaries is another crucial step for Type 9s in finding their voice. Boundaries not only protect their energy and space but also serve as a declaration of their individuality and needs. This act of self-assertion is a powerful statement of self-respect and an essential component of healthy interpersonal dynamics. Through the practice of setting boundaries, Type 9s learn to honor their peace, not by avoiding conflict, but by establishing clear lines of respect and understanding.

In conclusion, the journey towards self-assertion for Type 9s is both challenging and deeply rewarding. By embracing their inherent worth and learning to express their needs and set boundaries, Type 9s can achieve a more authentic and harmonious existence. The Enneagram, with its ancient wisdom and insights into human nature, serves as a guiding light on this journey, offering Type 9s the tools and understanding necessary to navigate the complexities of self-expression. As they find their voice, Type 9s not only enrich their own lives but also contribute to the greater tapestry of human connection, embodying the true essence of harmony and peace.

Strategies for Healthy Expression: Communication Strategies to Assert Needs While Maintaining Peace

In the journey toward self-discovery and personal growth, the Enneagram serves as a beacon, guiding individuals to understand their inner workings and navigate the complexities of interpersonal relationships. For Type 9 women, who naturally strive for peace and harmony, finding a balance between asserting their needs and maintaining their core value of peace can be particularly challenging. This section explores effective communication strategies that can empower Type 9 women to express themselves authentically while preserving the harmony they cherish.

Active Listening and Reflective Responses

One of the foundational steps in healthy communication is active listening, a skill that Type 9s often naturally excel at. By practicing active listening, not only do they validate the feelings and perspectives of others, but they also create a space where their own needs can be heard and respected. Reflective responses, which involve mirroring back what has been said, help in deepening understanding and ensuring that all parties feel understood. This technique fosters an environment of mutual respect, where Type 9s can feel more comfortable expressing their needs.

Assertive Communication

Assertive communication is key for Type 9s to express their needs and boundaries clearly and respectfully. This involves using "I" statements to own their feelings and express their needs without placing blame or making assumptions about others. For example, saying, "I feel overlooked when decisions are made without my input" instead of "You never consider what I want." Assertive communication allows Type 9s to assert their presence and needs while maintaining the respect and harmony they value.

Setting Boundaries with Compassion

For Type 9 women, setting boundaries is essential for healthy self-expression and personal well-being. However, the fear of causing conflict often holds them back. By framing boundaries as a means of maintaining their ability to contribute positively to relationships, Type 9s can align boundary-setting with their core values. Communicating boundaries with compassion, such as by explaining the reasons behind them and how they ultimately serve the relationship, can help in preserving harmony.

Negotiation and Compromise

Recognizing that not all situations can be resolved to everyone's complete satisfaction is crucial for Type 9s. Learning the art of negotiation and compromise—where their needs are part of the equation—is essential. This involves presenting their needs and desires as valid options to be considered alongside those of others. Negotiation skills enable Type 9s to find solutions that are acceptable to all parties, thus maintaining peace while ensuring their voices are heard.

Regular Self-Reflection

For Type 9s, regular self-reflection is vital in understanding their own needs, desires, and the tendencies that may prevent them from expressing them. Techniques such as journaling, meditation, or working with a therapist can provide insights into their inner world and help cultivate the courage to speak out. Self-reflection empowers Type 9s to understand the importance of their voice in the tapestry of their relationships.

Building a Support System

Surrounding themselves with supportive individuals who encourage and validate their expression can significantly bolster a Type 9's confidence in asserting their needs. A supportive environment reinforces the idea that their needs are important and that expressing them contributes to healthier and more fulfilling relationships.

while the path to finding and expressing one's voice can be daunting for Type 9 women, the Enneagram offers a map to navigate this journey. By employing these communication strategies, Type 9s can learn to assert their needs and express themselves more authentically, all while maintaining the harmony they deeply value. This balance is not only possible but essential for their growth and fulfillment, reflecting the Enneagram's timeless wisdom in fostering understanding and transformation within the rich diversity of human personality.

Beyond Merging: Relationships and Preserving Identity

Merging Patterns: Unraveling Type 9's Tendency to Lose Themselves in Relationships for Peace

In the intricate dance of relationships, Type 9 women often find themselves in a delicate balancing act, seeking harmony and peace at the expense of their own identity. This chapter delves into the phenomenon of merging patterns in Type 9s, a tendency to blend their desires, preferences, and even personalities with those of others to maintain tranquility and avoid conflict. Drawing from the rich historical context and profound insights of the Enneagram, we explore the roots of this pattern, its impact on relationships, and the journey towards preserving one's identity while fostering healthy connections.

The Nature of Merging

Merging, for Type 9s, is more than a habit; it's a survival strategy deeply embedded in their psyche. It stems from a core belief that their presence, needs, and opinions might disrupt the peace and stability of their relationships. This belief, often unconscious, leads to a pattern of behavior where the Type 9's identity becomes increasingly entwined with that of others, making it difficult for them to discern where their own desires end and others' begin. This tendency echoes the historical essence of the Enneagram, which seeks to harmonize various elements into a cohesive whole, much like Type 9s strive to create a seamless blend of their identity with those around them to preserve harmony.

The Cost of Peace

While the pursuit of peace is noble, for Type 9s, the cost can be high. The merging pattern can lead to a loss of self, where the Type 9's own goals, aspirations, and preferences are sidelined or completely forgotten. This self-abnegation, though it may stave off conflict in the short term, can result in a profound sense of emptiness and disconnection from one's self over time. It mirrors the Enneagram's journey through obscurity to self-discovery, highlighting the need for Type 9s to embark on a similar path of unearthing and asserting their true identity amidst the cacophony of external influences.

The Path to Authenticity

Breaking the pattern of merging requires conscious effort and self-awareness. It involves recognizing the value of one's own desires and the importance of expressing them within relationships. Type 9s must learn to navigate the fear of conflict, understanding that disagreement does not equate to disconnection. By actively engaging in practices that foster self-awareness—such as mindfulness, journaling, and the exploration of personal interests—Type 9s can begin to reclaim their identity and voice.

Communication as a Bridge

Effective communication is key to balancing the needs for peace and authenticity in relationships. Type 9s can practice expressing their needs and preferences clearly and assertively, using "I" statements to own their experiences without placing blame. This approach not only honors their own identity but also respects the autonomy and identity of their partners, fostering a relationship dynamic where both parties can thrive.

Seeking Support

The journey towards maintaining one's identity while nurturing healthy relationships can be challenging. Seeking support from therapists, coaches, or Enneagram groups can provide Type 9s with the tools and encouragement needed to navigate this path. These resources can offer insights into the dynamics of merging and strategies for developing a stronger sense of self within the context of relationships.

while the merging patterns of Type 9s stem from a deep-seated desire for harmony, recognizing and addressing this tendency is crucial for their personal growth and the health of their relationships. By exploring the roots of their merging behavior, engaging in self-awareness practices, and employing effective communication strategies, Type 9 women can forge a path towards a balanced and authentic existence. This journey, reflective of the Enneagram's own evolution, underscores the transformative power of self-knowledge and the pursuit of genuine connection, both with oneself and with others.

Healthy Boundaries: Crafting a Balanced Self in the Midst of Connection

In the intricate journey of self-discovery and interpersonal relationships, the art of maintaining healthy boundaries emerges as a pivotal theme for Type 9 women. Within the historical and philosophical context of the Enneagram, the evolution of understanding one's own boundaries reflects a deeper quest for balance between the self and the collective. This chapter explores strategies for Type 9 women to cultivate a sense of self while fostering fulfilling relationships, guided by the wisdom of the Enneagram's ancient teachings and its relevance to modern personal growth.

Understanding the Need for Boundaries

For Type 9 women, the concept of boundaries often poses a complex challenge. Their natural inclination towards peace and harmony may lead them to overlook their own needs, desires, and identity. However, just as the Enneagram teaches the importance of recognizing and embracing the distinct characteristics of each type, Type 9s must learn to acknowledge and honor their own boundaries as essential components of their well-being and personal identity. Boundaries, in this context, are not barriers but rather definitions that help Type 9s understand where they end and others begin, enabling them to engage in relationships with clarity and authenticity.

Strategies for Establishing Boundaries

Self-Reflection and Identification: The first step in establishing healthy boundaries is for Type 9s to engage in deep self-reflection, identifying their own needs, preferences, and values. Practices such as meditation, journaling, and the Enneagram's introspective tools can facilitate this process, helping Type 9s to uncover and articulate what truly matters to them.

Clear Communication: Once Type 9s have a firmer grasp on their own needs and boundaries, the next step is to communicate these clearly to others. Using "I" statements to express feelings and needs can be an effective way to assert boundaries without inciting conflict. For example, "I feel overwhelmed when I don't have time for myself. I need to ensure I have some quiet time each evening."

Practicing Assertiveness: Learning to say no is a critical aspect of maintaining healthy boundaries. Type 9s can practice assertiveness in small, manageable situations to build their confidence in asserting their needs without fear of disrupting harmony.

Seeking Support: Engaging with a supportive community, whether through Enneagram groups, therapy, or friendships, can provide Type 9s with encouragement and validation as they navigate the process of establishing and maintaining boundaries.

Regular Reassessment: Boundaries are not static; they may shift and evolve over time. Regular reassessment of one's needs and boundaries is crucial for Type 9s to ensure they remain relevant and reflective of their current state of being.

The Role of Boundaries in Preserving Identity

Healthy boundaries are instrumental in helping Type 9s preserve their identity within relationships. By defining and asserting their own needs and limits, Type 9s can engage more authentically with others, contributing to more meaningful and fulfilling relationships. Boundaries enable Type 9s to honor their own needs and identity without losing themselves in the process of merging with others. This balance between self and other reflects the Enneagram's broader teachings on the interplay between individuality and unity, offering a path towards true harmony and self-realization.

as Type 9 women embark on the journey of establishing healthy boundaries, they are guided by the timeless wisdom of the Enneagram. This ancient system, with its deep roots in spiritual and philosophical traditions, provides a framework for understanding the self in relation to others. Through the practice of setting boundaries, Type 9s learn to navigate the delicate balance between merging and maintaining their identity, fostering relationships that are both fulfilling and true to their essence. The path towards healthy boundaries is a journey of courage, self-awareness, and growth, leading Type 9 women towards a more balanced and authentic expression of themselves.

Chapter 5:

Presence and Stillness: Finding Your Calm

Tapping into Inner Peace: The Type 9 Woman's Natural Reservoir of Calmness

In the intricate landscape of the Enneagram, Type 9 women stand as beacons of calm and serenity, navigating the world with a grace that belies the depth of their inner peace. This chapter delves into the essence of the Type 9 woman's natural reservoir of calmness, exploring how this intrinsic tranquility not only defines their interactions with the world but also serves as a foundation for their personal growth and wellbeing. Drawing from the rich historical tapestry of the Enneagram, we uncover the spiritual and philosophical roots of Type 9's inherent peace, offering insights into how they can harness this gift to lead a life of balanced serenity and presence.

The Essence of Calmness in Type 9s

Type 9 women are endowed with an innate ability to remain centered amidst the chaos of life. This calmness is not merely an absence of disturbance but a profound state of being, deeply rooted in their core. It is a manifestation of their desire for harmony and unity, reflecting the Enneagram's ancient teachings on balance and the interconnectedness of all things. Just as the Enneagram has evolved through centuries, incorporating wisdom from diverse traditions to guide individuals towards self-knowledge, Type 9s embody this integration, drawing from their inner well of peace to navigate life's complexities with grace.

Harnessing Inner Peace

For Type 9 women, tapping into their natural calm requires mindfulness and intentionality. It involves cultivating a practice of presence, where they consciously engage with the present moment, embracing their experiences without judgment. This practice of presence can be nurtured through meditation, yoga, or simply spending quiet time in nature. These activities not only reinforce their connection to their inner peace but also help them to recognize when they are drifting away from their center, allowing them to realign with their core essence.

The Role of Stillness

Stillness plays a crucial role in the Type 9 woman's journey towards inner peace. In stillness, Type 9s find the space to listen to their inner voice, a voice often drowned out by the noise of their peacemaking efforts. Embracing stillness allows Type 9s to connect with their desires, dreams, and aspirations, giving them the clarity to pursue a life that is true to themselves. This stillness can be cultivated through practices such as mindfulness meditation, reflective journaling, or any activity that encourages inner contemplation and awareness.

Overcoming Obstacles to Inner Peace

While the path to tapping into their inner peace is natural for Type 9s, it is not without its challenges. The tendency to merge with others can lead to a disconnection from their own needs and desires, obscuring their inner calm. Recognizing and addressing this tendency is crucial for Type 9s to maintain their sense of self and inner peace. Setting boundaries, engaging in self-reflection, and prioritizing self-care are essential strategies for overcoming these obstacles, enabling Type 9s to stay connected to their inner reservoir of calmness.

The Power of Inner Peace

The inner peace of Type 9 women is a powerful force, offering them resilience in the face of adversity and enabling them to act as sources of calm and stability for those around them. By tapping into their natural calmness, Type 9s can navigate life's challenges with equanimity, fostering environments of peace and harmony wherever they go. Their journey of maintaining presence and stillness is a testament to the enduring wisdom of the Enneagram, guiding Type 9s towards a life of authenticity, fulfillment, and profound serenity.

the Type 9 woman's journey to tapping into her inner peace is both a personal quest and a reflection of the Enneagram's ancient teachings. By embracing their natural reservoir of calmness, cultivating stillness, and overcoming the obstacles that obscure their inner peace, Type 9s can unlock the full potential of their serene essence. In doing so, they not only enrich their own lives but also contribute to the collective harmony of the world around them, embodying the timeless wisdom of the Enneagram in their pursuit of balanced and peaceful existence.

Mindfulness Techniques: Cultivating Inner Peace and Presence for the Type 9 Woman

In the journey towards inner peace and presence, mindfulness stands as a pillar for those seeking to deepen their understanding of self and to cultivate a serene state of being. For Type 9 women, the practice of mindfulness offers a pathway to enhance their natural reservoir of calmness, enabling them to navigate the world with greater equanimity and awareness. This chapter presents a series of meditations and practices specifically tailored to the needs of Type 9 women, drawing on the rich historical and philosophical foundations of the Enneagram to guide them towards a more profound sense of inner peace and presence.

Grounding Meditation

A grounding meditation is particularly beneficial for Type 9 women, helping them to reconnect with their core self and to remain present amidst the ever-changing dynamics of life. This practice involves sitting or lying down in a comfortable position and focusing on the sensation of the body making contact with the ground. By visualizing roots growing from their body into the earth, Type 9s can foster a sense of stability and groundedness, reminding them of their strength and resilience.

Breathing Exercises

Breath is a powerful tool for centering the mind and body, and breathing exercises can be incredibly effective in managing stress and fostering inner peace. A simple technique involves focusing on the breath, inhaling deeply through the nose for a count of four, holding the breath for a count of seven, and exhaling slowly through the mouth for a count of eight. This practice, known as the 4-7-8 breathing technique, can help Type 9s to slow down their thought processes and to bring their attention back to the present moment.

Walking Meditation

Walking meditation combines the physical activity of walking with the mindful practice of meditation, offering Type 9 women a dynamic way to cultivate presence. This practice involves walking slowly and deliberately, paying close attention to the sensation of each footstep and the rhythm of the breath. By engaging in walking meditation, Type 9s can enjoy the benefits of mindfulness while also experiencing the restorative power of movement.

Journaling for Self-Discovery

Journaling is a reflective practice that allows Type 9 women to explore their thoughts, feelings, and experiences in a structured and contemplative manner. By setting aside time each day to write in a journal, Type 9s can gain insights into their inner world, identifying patterns of thought and behavior that may be hindering their sense of peace and presence. This practice encourages self-exploration and personal growth, providing Type 9s with a tangible way to track their journey towards inner calm.

Gratitude Practice

Cultivating gratitude is a powerful mindfulness technique that can shift the focus from what is lacking to what is abundant in one's life. For Type 9 women, practicing gratitude involves taking time each day to reflect on and appreciate the positive aspects of their lives, whether it be relationships, personal achievements, or simple pleasures. By focusing on gratitude, Type 9s can enhance their overall sense of well-being and foster a more positive and present mindset.

the mindfulness techniques outlined in this chapter offer Type 9 women practical and accessible ways to enhance their natural calmness and presence. By incorporating these practices into their daily routines, Type 9s can deepen their connection to themselves and to the world around them, embodying the essence of the Enneagram's teachings on self-knowledge and personal growth. Through mindfulness, Type 9 women can navigate the complexities of life with grace and serenity, cultivating an inner peace that radiates outward, enriching their relationships and their experience of the world.

Chapter 6:

Conquering Inertia: Motivation and Taking Action

Understanding Apathy: The Peaceful Path and Its Unintended Consequences

Within the diverse spectrum of human personality, Type 9s of the Enneagram embody a quest for peace and harmony that is as admirable as it is challenging. This chapter explores the subtle intricacies of how the Type 9's core desire for peace can, paradoxically, usher them into states of procrastination and passivity. Drawing from the Enneagram's profound historical roots and its evolution as a tool for deep self-knowledge, we unravel the dynamics behind Type 9s' apathy, offering insights into overcoming inertia to embrace a more motivated and action-oriented life.

The Paradox of Peace

Type 9s are the archetypal peacemakers of the Enneagram, with a natural inclination toward maintaining harmony in their surroundings. Their aversion to conflict and deep-seated belief in the value of a tranquil existence drive them to seek consensus and accommodate others' needs often at the expense of their own. However, this commendable pursuit of peace can inadvertently lead to a state of inertia, where the avoidance of conflict and decision-making results in procrastination and passivity. This paradox reflects the historical essence of the Enneagram itself, which teaches that each type's greatest strength can also be its most significant challenge.

Apathy as a Defense Mechanism

For Type 9s, apathy is not merely a lack of interest or laziness but a subconscious defense mechanism to avoid the discomfort of discord and upheaval. It manifests as an internal withdrawal from their own desires and aspirations, a peacekeeping strategy that ensures the external environment remains undisturbed. This withdrawal, while effective in avoiding immediate conflict, can lead to long-term dissatisfaction and unfulfillment, as the Type 9's own goals and potential remain unrealized.

The Cost of Silence

The silent cost of this peace-at-all-costs approach is a life not fully lived. Type 9s may find themselves on the periphery of their existence, observers rather than active participants in their own stories. This state of inertia stifles their growth, creativity, and ability to effect change in their lives and the world around them. The teachings of the Enneagram, deeply rooted in ancient wisdom, highlight the importance of confronting one's fears and challenges as a pathway to true growth and self-discovery.

Strategies for Overcoming Inertia

To conquer inertia, Type 9s are encouraged to engage in practices that foster self-awareness and assertiveness. Setting small, achievable goals can help build the momentum needed to break out of passive states. Mindfulness and meditation can enhance present-moment awareness, allowing Type 9s to recognize and gently challenge their avoidance patterns. Assertiveness training can empower them to express their needs and desires, confronting the fear of conflict in a constructive manner.

Embracing Action and Change

The journey toward action and change involves embracing the discomfort that comes with growth. Type 9s can learn to view conflict not as a threat to peace but as an opportunity for deeper understanding and authentic connection. By actively participating in their own lives, making decisions, and taking risks, Type 9s can transform their desire for peace into a dynamic force for positive change, both within themselves and in their interactions with the world.

In conclusion, understanding and overcoming the apathy associated with the Type 9's desire for peace is a profound journey of self-discovery and empowerment. By engaging with the Enneagram's historical wisdom and applying practical strategies for action, Type 9 women can move beyond inertia, embracing a life of motivated intention and fulfilling engagement. This chapter not only highlights the challenges faced by Type 9s but also celebrates their potential for growth, encouraging them to step into their power and manifest their inner peace into outward action.

Strategies for Motivation: Empowering Type 9 Women to Set Goals and Take Action

In the labyrinth of human personality, Type 9 women of the Enneagram are often seen as the embodiment of calm and harmony. Yet, beneath this serene exterior lies a challenge deeply rooted in their quest for peace: the battle against inertia. Drawing from the Enneagram's ancient wisdom and its journey through history as a tool for profound self-knowledge, this chapter aims to arm Type 9 women with practical strategies for motivation, setting goals, and initiating action. These tools are not just steps but bridges connecting their inner world of peace with the outer world of dynamic engagement.

Creating a Vision Board

A vision board is a tangible representation of one's goals and aspirations. For Type 9 women, who may struggle with defining their own desires, creating a vision board can serve as a powerful tool for self-discovery and motivation. By selecting images and words that resonate with their true wishes for their lives, Type 9s can externalize and clarify their goals, making them more tangible and actionable.

The Power of Incremental Goals

Setting large, ambitious goals can be overwhelming, particularly for Type 9s, who might fear the upheaval change can bring. Breaking down larger goals into smaller, manageable tasks can help mitigate this fear, making the process of achieving goals feel less daunting and more achievable. Each small victory builds momentum, gradually overcoming inertia and reinforcing the belief in their ability to effect change.

Establishing Routines

Routine can be a powerful ally for Type 9s, providing a structured framework that encourages consistent action. Establishing a daily or weekly routine that includes time dedicated to working towards their goals can help Type 9s turn intention into action. Within this structure, it's important to include flexibility to adjust as needed, ensuring that the routine supports their goals without becoming a source of stress.

Mindfulness and Reflection

Mindfulness practices, such as meditation or journaling, can help Type 9 women stay connected to their inner motivations and desires. Regular reflection allows them to monitor their progress, reassess their goals, and recognize any patterns of procrastination or avoidance. This self-awareness is crucial in maintaining motivation and ensuring that their actions align with their true self.

Seeking Accountability

For Type 9s, sharing their goals with a trusted friend or family member can provide an external source of motivation and accountability. Knowing that someone else is aware of their goals and may ask about their progress can be a powerful motivator. Additionally, engaging with a mentor or joining a group with similar goals can offer support, encouragement, and valuable insights.

Celebrating Progress

Acknowledging and celebrating each step forward, no matter how small, is vital for maintaining motivation. Type 9 women should be encouraged to recognize their efforts and successes along the way, treating themselves with kindness and appreciation. Celebrating progress reinforces positive behavior and builds confidence, fueling further action towards their goals.

In weaving these strategies into the fabric of their lives, Type 9 women can transform the challenge of inertia into a journey of empowerment. By setting clear goals, taking incremental steps, and embracing their inherent capacity for growth and change, they can move from a state of passivity to one of active engagement with the world. The wisdom of the Enneagram, with its deep roots in ancient spiritual and philosophical traditions, serves as a guiding light on this journey, offering insights and practices that support Type 9 women in realizing their full potential and living a life of purpose, action, and fulfillment.

Chapter 7:

Awakening Your Energy: Movement and Reconnection

Movement as Medicine: Harnessing Exercise and Embodied Practices to Overcome Type 9 Inertia and Cultivate Vibrancy

In the realm of personal growth and self-discovery, the journey of the Type 9 woman is one marked by a quest for peace, harmony, and inner balance. Yet, this quest is often met with the challenge of inertia—a state of rest that, while comfortable, can hinder the dynamic flow of life's energies and the pursuit of vibrant health. This chapter delves into the transformative power of movement as medicine, exploring how exercise and embodied practices can serve as vital tools for Type 9 women to counteract inertia, reinvigorate their energy, and reconnect with their physical and emotional selves. Drawing from the ancient wisdom of the Enneagram and its rich historical and philosophical roots, we uncover strategies for awakening the dormant energy within, guiding Type 9s toward a more active, engaged, and vibrant existence.

The Importance of Physical Movement

For Type 9 women, the tendency towards inertia is not merely a physical phenomenon but an emotional and spiritual one as well. Physical movement, therefore, becomes a conduit for breaking through layers of passivity, igniting the spark of vitality that resides within. Exercise and physical activities—be it yoga, dance, walking, or any form of movement that resonates—act as a bridge, reconnecting Type 9s with their bodies and the present moment. This reconnection is crucial, as it awakens them to the joys and sensations of life, encouraging a more engaged and active participation in their own journey.

Embodied Practices for Inner Harmony

Embodied practices such as yoga and Tai Chi offer more than just physical exercise; they are forms of moving meditation that harmonize the body, mind, and spirit. For Type 9s, these practices provide a dual benefit: they counter physical inertia while also promoting mental and emotional well-being. The slow, deliberate movements and focus on breathwork inherent in these practices foster a sense of inner calm and balance, aligning perfectly with the Type 9's desire for peace. Moreover, these activities encourage mindfulness, a quality that helps Type 9s become more aware of their tendencies towards passivity and avoidance, empowering them to make conscious choices towards action and presence.

Reconnecting Through Nature

Engagement with the natural world offers another powerful avenue for Type 9s to awaken their energy and combat inertia. Activities such as hiking, gardening, or simply spending time in nature can be profoundly rejuvenating, grounding Type 9s in the physical world and reminding them of the interconnectedness of all life. The natural environment provides a sense of calm and stability, while also inspiring movement and exploration, helping Type 9s to break free from the confines of inertia and rediscover their innate vibrancy.

Creating a Personal Movement Ritual

For Type 9 women, establishing a personal movement ritual can be a meaningful way to integrate physical activity into their daily lives. This ritual doesn't have to be rigorous or time-consuming; it simply needs to be consistent and enjoyable, something that they look forward to each day. Whether it's a morning walk, a dance session, or a series of stretches, the key is in the regularity and the intention behind the action—the intention to nurture their body, honor their need for movement, and cultivate energy and presence.

Overcoming Barriers to Movement

Understanding and addressing the psychological barriers that contribute to inertia is crucial for Type 9s. This may involve setting manageable goals, seeking support from friends or a community, and gently challenging the inner critic that deters them from action. Recognizing that movement is not just a physical activity but a form of self-care and self-respect can also be a powerful motivator, shifting the perspective from one of obligation to one of personal empowerment.

Type 9 women, the journey towards overcoming inertia and cultivating vibrancy is deeply intertwined with the practice of movement and physical engagement. By embracing exercise and embodied practices as forms of medicine, Type 9s can unlock the door to a more dynamic, engaged, and vibrant life. This path of movement and reconnection not only aligns with the teachings of the Enneagram but also embodies the timeless wisdom that true peace and harmony are found not in stillness but in the joyous embrace of life's perpetual dance.

Finding Joy in Movement: Embracing Gentle Forms of Exercise for Type 9s

For Type 9 women, embarking on a journey to awaken their energy and reconnect with their essence, the key lies not in the intensity of movement but in the joy and connection it brings. This chapter explores various forms of movement that resonate with the Type 9's desire for harmony and inner peace, emphasizing activities that nurture rather than deplete, and connect rather than force. Drawing upon the Enneagram's deep historical roots and its message of self-discovery, we identify practices that align with the Type 9's natural rhythm, encouraging them to find joy and vibrancy in gentle, yet profoundly transformative, forms of movement.

Yoga: The Path to Inner Balance

Yoga stands out as a quintessential practice for Type 9 women, offering a blend of physical movement, breath control, and meditation. The gentle flow of yoga aligns with the Type 9's preference for non-confrontational and harmonious activities, providing a space for them to connect with their bodies and minds in a peaceful manner. The practice of yoga encourages presence and mindfulness, allowing Type 9s to gently awaken their dormant energies and rediscover the joy of movement in a supportive and nurturing environment.

Tai Chi: Moving Meditation for Harmony

Tai Chi, an ancient martial art known for its slow and graceful movements, offers Type 9s a powerful way to cultivate energy and balance. Described as meditation in motion, Tai Chi focuses on the flow of chi (energy) through the body, promoting physical health, mental clarity, and emotional calmness. This practice aligns with the Type 9's desire for peace and connection, providing a gentle yet effective pathway to increase vitality and reduce stress.

Nature Walks: Reconnecting with the Earth

For Type 9 women, spending time in nature can be incredibly rejuvenating and grounding. Engaging in regular nature walks invites a sense of connection with the earth and the larger web of life, offering a profound sense of belonging and peace. Walking in natural settings, whether in a park, by the sea, or in the mountains, allows Type 9s to move their bodies in a gentle, rhythmic manner, fostering a deep reconnection with their own nature and the world around them.

Dance: Expressive Freedom and Joy

Dance, in its many forms, provides a unique opportunity for Type 9s to explore and express their inner world through movement. Whether it's structured dance forms like ballroom or free-form movement to their favorite music, dancing invites Type 9s to experience the joy of expressing themselves authentically. Dance encourages spontaneity and creativity, helping Type 9s to break free from inertia and experience the exhilaration of being fully present and alive in their bodies.

Swimming: Fluidity and Ease

Swimming offers another form of gentle, yet effective, movement that can be particularly beneficial for Type 9 women. The buoyancy of water provides a sense of weightlessness and ease, reducing the impact on joints and allowing for a fluid, resistance-based form of exercise. Swimming laps or simply enjoying the sensation of moving through water can be meditative, helping Type 9s to feel more connected to their bodies and the calming element of water.

Type 9 women, finding joy in movement is about embracing activities that resonate with their core values of peace, harmony, and connection. By choosing forms of exercise that emphasize gentleness, mindfulness, and joy, Type 9s can awaken their energy and rediscover the vibrancy of life. These practices not only counteract inertia but also serve as powerful tools for personal growth and self-discovery, reflecting the timeless wisdom of the Enneagram in fostering a deeper connection with oneself and the world.

Chapter 8:

Self-Care for the Peacemaker: Rest and Restoration

Combating Self-Neglect: Prioritizing Self in the Service of Harmony

In the rich tapestry of Enneagram personalities, Type 9 women embody the essence of peace and harmony, often serving as the cornerstone of stability in their communities and relationships. However, this noble pursuit comes with its pitfalls, the most significant of which is a tendency towards self-neglect. This chapter delves into the critical issue of self-care for Type 9 women, addressing the deeply ingrained habit of prioritizing others' needs at the expense of their own well-being. Drawing on the profound historical and philosophical underpinnings of the Enneagram, we explore strategies for Type 9s to balance their altruistic tendencies with essential self-care practices, ensuring their own needs are met while continuing to nurture peace around them.

Understanding the Root of Self-Neglect

For Type 9 women, the inclination to merge with the preferences, desires, and needs of those around them is not merely a habit but a deeply rooted survival strategy. This strategy, while effective in maintaining external harmony, often leads to internal dissonance and neglect of personal needs, health, and aspirations. The historical development of the Enneagram illuminates the complexity of Type 9's motivations, tracing back to ancient philosophies that emphasize the interconnectedness of all beings. However, these teachings also underscore the importance of individual well-being as the foundation for true harmony and peace.

The Art of Saying 'No'

Learning to assert boundaries and comfortably say 'no' is a crucial step for Type 9 women in combating self-neglect. This skill allows them to honor their own needs and limitations without feeling guilty for not acquiescing to every request or expectation. Assertiveness training, guided by the principles of the Enneagram, can help Type 9s recognize their worth and the legitimacy of their needs, empowering them to make choices that align with their well-being.

Establishing a Self-Care Routine

A personalized self-care routine is vital for Type 9 women to recharge and maintain their inner reservoir of peace. This routine can include practices such as regular physical activity, mindful meditation, engaging in hobbies, and ensuring adequate rest. By setting aside dedicated time for these activities, Type 9s can cultivate a sense of self-connection and rejuvenation, enabling them to approach their peacemaking roles with renewed vigor and clarity.

Embracing Solo Time for Reflection

Solo time for reflection allows Type 9s to reconnect with their inner selves, exploring their desires, dreams, and feelings without external influence. This practice of solitude can be facilitated through journaling, nature walks, or quiet contemplation. It serves as a reminder to Type 9 women that their identity and needs are distinct and valuable, deserving of attention and care.

Seeking Supportive Relationships

While Type 9s are adept at providing support, they too need a network of understanding and encouraging individuals who can remind them of the importance of self-care. Cultivating relationships with those who recognize and respect their need for self-care can provide Type 9 women with the external accountability and encouragement necessary to prioritize their well-being.

Type 9 women, the journey toward self-care is both a challenge and an opportunity for growth. By addressing the tendency towards self-neglect, they can ensure that their pursuit of harmony and peace is not at their expense. The wisdom of the Enneagram, with its deep roots in ancient teachings and its nuanced understanding of personality dynamics, offers invaluable guidance for Type 9s on this path. Through deliberate self-care practices, Type 9 women can preserve their own well-being while continuing to be beacons of peace and stability for those around them. This balance is not only possible but essential for their fulfillment and effectiveness as peacemakers.

Restorative Practices: Replenishing the Type 9's Reservoir of Peace

In the quest for inner harmony and balance, Type 9 women of the Enneagram often extend themselves in service to others, sometimes at the cost of their own well-being. The ancient wisdom of the Enneagram, with its roots deeply embedded in spiritual and philosophical soil, offers a map for these peacemakers to navigate back to their center, emphasizing the critical role of rest and restorative practices in maintaining their energy and nurturing inner peace. This chapter explores self-care techniques specifically tailored to rejuvenate Type 9s, enabling them to sustain their altruistic endeavors without depleting their own reserves.

The Vitality of Rest

For Type 9s, rest is not a luxury but a necessity. It is the foundation upon which their energy and peace are built. Quality sleep, periods of relaxation, and moments of stillness throughout the day are essential practices that allow Type 9s to disconnect from external demands and reconnect with their inner selves. Embracing rest as a priority ensures that Type 9s can approach their daily lives with renewed vigor and a clear mind, ready to engage with the world from a place of strength rather than from depletion.

Mindful Meditation

Mindful meditation offers a pathway for Type 9s to cultivate a deep sense of inner peace, counteracting the noise and distractions that often lead to fragmentation and loss of self. Through practices such as focused breathing, guided imagery, or silent reflection, Type 9s can explore the landscapes of their inner world, encountering a tranquility that replenishes their spirit. This practice of intentional stillness helps Type 9s to anchor themselves in the present moment, fostering a resilient foundation of calmness amidst life's turbulence.

Gentle Yoga

Gentle yoga, with its emphasis on slow movements, breath work, and mindful awareness, aligns perfectly with the Type 9's natural inclination towards harmony and balance. This form of exercise not only rejuvenates the body but also quiets the mind, allowing Type 9s to release tension, restore energy, and nurture a deep sense of well-being. Integrating gentle yoga into their self-care routine offers Type 9s a holistic approach to maintaining their health and inner peace.

Nature Immersion

Immersing themselves in nature is a powerful restorative practice for Type 9s. The natural world, with its inherent harmony and rhythm, resonates deeply with Type 9s, providing a sanctuary from the demands of everyday life. Activities such as walking in a park, sitting by a stream, or simply being outdoors can be profoundly rejuvenating for Type 9s, offering them a sense of connection to the larger web of life and a reminder of the peace that exists within and around them.

Creative Expression

Engaging in creative activities such as painting, writing, gardening, or playing music can be a form of restorative self-care for Type 9s. These activities provide an outlet for expressing inner thoughts and feelings, facilitating a journey of self-discovery and personal growth. Through creative expression, Type 9s can explore aspects of themselves that may be neglected in their pursuit of peace, finding joy and fulfillment in the act of creation.

Type 9 women, the journey towards self-care is a journey back to themselves. By embracing restorative practices such as rest, mindful meditation, gentle yoga, nature immersion, and creative expression, Type 9s can replenish their energy, nurture their inner peace, and sustain their capacity to bring harmony to the world. The ancient teachings of the Enneagram, with its deep understanding of the human psyche, serve as a guide for Type 9s in this journey, reminding them that true peace begins with caring for oneself. Through dedicated self-care, Type 9s can continue to serve as beacons of peace, grounded in their own well-being and radiating tranquility to all they encounter.

Creating a Nourishing Environment: Cultivating Peaceful Spaces for the Type 9 Woman

For Type 9 women, who naturally seek harmony and tranquility, the environment in which they reside and spend time significantly influences their inner peace and well-being. This chapter delves into the art of creating a nourishing home space, a sanctuary that supports relaxation and rejuvenation for the Type 9 woman. Drawing on the Enneagram's ancient wisdom and its emphasis on personal growth and self-awareness, we explore practical and soulful strategies to design environments that resonate with Type 9's core need for peace, facilitating a deeper connection with themselves and enhancing their capacity for rest and restoration.

The Essence of a Peaceful Home

A peaceful home for a Type 9 goes beyond mere aesthetics; it's a space that reflects their innermost desires for calm and serenity. This involves creating an environment that not only appeals to the senses but also supports their inherent need to withdraw and recharge. Elements such as soft lighting, soothing colors, and natural materials can profoundly impact a Type 9's sense of peace, making their home a true reflection of their quest for harmony.

Personal Sanctuaries

Every Type 9 woman benefits from having a personal sanctuary—a space dedicated solely to relaxation and introspection. This could be a cozy corner with comfortable seating, surrounded by books, plants, and personal mementos that inspire peace and contemplation. In this personal sanctuary, Type 9s can engage in practices such as meditation, reading, or simply being, allowing them to disconnect from the world's demands and reconnect with their inner selves.

Nature Indoors

Incorporating elements of nature into the home environment can have a soothing effect on Type 9s, who often feel a deep connection to the natural world. Indoor plants, natural light, and even nature sounds can create an atmosphere that promotes relaxation and well-being. These elements remind Type 9s of the beauty and peace that exist in the world, encouraging a sense of groundedness and present-moment awareness.

Clutter-Free Spaces

For Type 9s, a cluttered environment can lead to a cluttered mind, hindering their ability to relax fully. Adopting a minimalist approach, focusing on simplicity and functionality, can help in maintaining a clutter-free space. Regularly decluttering and organizing the home ensures that the environment remains conducive to relaxation, allowing Type 9s to enjoy their surroundings without the distraction of unnecessary items.

Harmony in Relationships

Creating a nourishing environment also involves fostering harmony in relationships within the home. Open communication, shared responsibilities, and mutual respect ensure that the home remains a sanctuary for all occupants. Type 9s, in particular, can encourage these practices, promoting an atmosphere of peace and cooperation that aligns with their core values.

Chapter 9:

Handling Anger: Healthy Expression for the Peacemaker

Hidden Anger: Navigating the Type 9's Path to Peaceful Resolution

For Type 9 women, the Enneagram offers profound insights into their harmonious nature and the underlying challenges they face with anger. Historically, the Enneagram has served as a mirror reflecting the complexities of human emotions and motivations. In the case of Type 9s, their aversion to conflict and deep-seated desire for peace often lead them to suppress or minimize their anger. This chapter delves into the nuanced dynamics of how Type 9s handle anger, exploring strategies for acknowledging and expressing this powerful emotion in ways that are healthy and constructive, while maintaining their core values of peace and harmony.

The Nature of Suppressed Anger

Type 9s are known for their peacemaking abilities, often going to great lengths to maintain harmony in their relationships and environment. However, this commendable trait comes with its pitfalls. In their quest to avoid conflict, Type 9s may inadvertently suppress their anger, storing it away like hidden treasures locked in a chest. Over time, this unacknowledged anger can simmer beneath the surface, manifesting in passive-aggressive behavior, resentment, or a pervasive sense of dissatisfaction. The ancient wisdom of the Enneagram teaches us that acknowledging our shadows is the first step toward growth and self-awareness.

Understanding Anger as a Messenger

Anger, in its essence, is a messenger. For Type 9s, learning to listen to the message anger brings can be a transformative process. Rather than viewing anger as a disruptor of peace, it can be seen as an indicator of unmet needs, boundaries being crossed, or values being challenged. By reframing anger as a signal rather than a threat, Type 9s can begin to address the underlying issues that give rise to this emotion, facilitating a healthier expression of their needs and desires.

Practices for Acknowledging Anger

Mindfulness and self-reflection are crucial practices for Type 9s to become more attuned to their feelings of anger. Techniques such as journaling can provide a safe outlet for exploring these emotions, allowing Type 9s to express their anger without fear of judgment or conflict. Mindfulness meditation can also help Type 9s to observe their anger without immediately reacting, creating space for understanding and compassionate self-inquiry.

Expressing Anger Constructively

Constructive expression of anger is key to resolving the internal conflict Type 9s experience. Communication skills such as using "I" statements allow Type 9s to express their feelings and needs directly and assertively, reducing the likelihood of misunderstandings. For example, saying "I feel overlooked when my opinions are not considered" directly addresses the issue without placing blame. Learning to express anger in the moment, rather than letting it build up, can also prevent resentment and promote healthier relationships.

Seeking Support

Navigating the complex terrain of anger can be challenging for Type 9s. Seeking support from a therapist, counselor, or Enneagram coach can provide valuable insights and strategies for dealing with anger in a healthy manner. Support groups or workshops focused on emotional intelligence and communication can also offer guidance and encouragement for Type 9s on their journey to healthier emotional expression.

Identifying Anger Triggers: Uncovering the Roots of Suppressed Emotions

For Type 9 women, navigating the landscape of their emotions, particularly anger, requires a journey into self-awareness that the Enneagram facilitates with profound depth. This chapter focuses on identifying situations and behaviors that often spark suppressed anger in Type 9s, aiming to equip them with the understanding needed to address and express their feelings constructively. Drawing from the historical and philosophical richness of the Enneagram, we explore practical ways for Type 9 women to recognize their anger triggers, offering a foundation for healthier emotional expression and personal growth.

Understanding Anger in Type 9s

Type 9s' quest for peace often leads them to suppress their anger, fearing that its expression might disrupt harmony. However, unrecognized and unaddressed anger can erode this sought-after peace from within. The Enneagram's teachings, steeped in centuries of wisdom, highlight the importance of embracing all facets of our emotions as a pathway to true self-knowledge and harmony.

Common Anger Triggers for Type 9s

Feeling Overlooked or Ignored: Type 9s value being part of a collective but may find themselves fading into the background, leading to feelings of invisibility and, subsequently, resentment.

Having Their Boundaries Overstepped: While often flexible, Type 9s do have limits. Repeated disregard for their boundaries can spark deep-seated anger.

Disruption of Personal Peace: Situations that threaten their inner tranquility, such as conflict or chaos, can be significant triggers.

Unacknowledged Contributions: Type 9s contribute to their environments in quiet, substantial ways. Lack of recognition can lead to feelings of underappreciation and anger.

Pressure to Conform: Being coerced into decisions or actions that conflict with their values or desires can ignite a slow burn of resentment in Type 9s.

Strategies for Identifying Triggers

Reflective Journaling: Regularly writing about daily experiences and emotional responses can help Type 9s track patterns and identify specific triggers of anger.

Mindfulness Practices: Engaging in mindfulness can enhance Type 9s' awareness of their emotional state, helping them recognize the onset of anger and its triggers in real-time.

Seek Feedback: Sometimes, external perspectives can illuminate blind spots. Conversations with trusted friends or family about when they've observed anger can provide valuable insights.

Body Awareness Exercises: Type 9s may first notice anger in their bodies (e.g., tension, restlessness). Body scanning and other somatic practices can help in recognizing these physical cues as signs of suppressed anger.

Therapy or Counseling: Professional guidance can offer a structured approach to exploring and understanding anger, providing tools for managing emotions effectively.

Identifying anger triggers is an essential step toward healthy emotional expression and personal harmony. By acknowledging and addressing these triggers, Type 9s can navigate their path to peace with authenticity and resilience. The ancient wisdom of the Enneagram, with its nuanced understanding of personality dynamics, offers a guiding light on this journey, encouraging Type 9s to embrace their full emotional spectrum. In doing so, they not only honor their own well-being but also enrich their contributions to the harmony they seek to create in the world.

Strategies for Expressing Anger: Balancing Honesty with Harmony

For Type 9 women, the harmonious peacemakers of the Enneagram, expressing anger can feel antithetical to their core identity. Their natural inclination towards maintaining peace often leads them to suppress or minimize their anger, fearing that its expression might disturb the tranquility they cherish. However, the ancient wisdom of the Enneagram teaches us that true peace is not the absence of conflict but the presence of authenticity and understanding. This chapter explores constructive ways for Type 9 women to express their anger without compromising their innate peacemaking instincts, drawing on the Enneagram's rich historical and philosophical insights to navigate the delicate balance between honesty and harmony.

Embrace Anger as a Tool for Self-Awareness

The first step in expressing anger constructively is to recognize it as a valid and valuable emotion. For Type 9s, anger can serve as a critical indicator of personal boundaries being crossed or needs not being met. By viewing anger through the lens of self-awareness, Type 9 women can begin to understand its root causes and address the underlying issues rather than the emotion itself. This perspective aligns with the Enneagram's emphasis on personal growth and the integration of all aspects of the self.

Mindful Communication

When expressing anger, mindful communication is key. Type 9s should aim to articulate their feelings clearly and calmly, using "I" statements to take ownership of their emotions and avoid placing blame. For example, instead of saying, "You always ignore my opinions," a Type 9 might say, "I feel hurt when my opinions aren't considered." This approach facilitates open dialogue and fosters understanding, allowing Type 9 women to express their anger while maintaining the relationship's integrity.

Scheduled Conversations

For Type 9s, spontaneous confrontations can be overwhelming. Scheduling a specific time to discuss grievances can provide a sense of control and preparation, making it easier for them to articulate their thoughts and feelings. This method ensures that both parties are mentally and emotionally prepared for the conversation, increasing the likelihood of a productive and harmonious outcome.

Seeking Mediation

In situations where direct expression feels too daunting, seeking the assistance of a mediator can be beneficial. A trusted friend, family member, or professional counselor can provide the support and objectivity needed to navigate difficult conversations. This intermediary can help ensure that the Type 9's voice is heard and their anger is expressed in a constructive manner.

Practicing Self-Compassion

Expressing anger is a challenging process for Type 9 women, and it's essential to approach it with self-compassion. Acknowledging the effort it takes to step out of their comfort zone and affirming their right to express their emotions can bolster their confidence and resilience. Self-compassion reinforces the understanding that seeking peace does not mean neglecting one's own needs and feelings.

learning to express anger constructively is an essential component of their journey towards authenticity and personal fulfillment. By embracing anger as a tool for self-awareness, engaging in mindful communication, preparing for conversations, seeking mediation when necessary, and practicing self-compassion, Type 9s can navigate the complexities of their emotions without compromising their peacemaking essence. The teachings of the Enneagram, with its deep roots in ancient wisdom, offer invaluable guidance on this path, encouraging Type 9 women to embrace their full emotional spectrum in pursuit of true harmony and understanding.

Chapter 10:

Unveiling Your Wings: Exploring the Nuances of Your Personality

Understanding Wings: The Dual Influences Shaping the Type 9 Personality

The Enneagram, a system rich in history and depth, offers not just a window into our core personalities but also insights into the nuanced variations that make each of us unique. For Type 9 women, known for their peace-seeking nature and aversion to conflict, the concept of "wings" introduces a compelling layer of complexity to their personality profile. This chapter explores the wings adjacent to Type 9—Type 8 (the Challenger) and Type 1 (the Reformer)—and how these influences manifest in the Type 9w8 (more assertive) and Type 9w1 (more introspective) variations, shaping their approach to life, relationships, and personal growth.

The 9w8: The Comfort Seeker Meets the Challenger

Type 9s with an 8 wing (9w8) embody a unique blend of the Type 9's desire for peace and the Type 8's assertive, sometimes confrontational, nature. This combination results in individuals who, while inherently valuing harmony, are not afraid to assert themselves or take charge when necessary. The 9w8s possess a quiet strength, an ability to stand firm, and advocate for themselves and others without compromising their core need for inner and outer peace.

The presence of the 8 wing lends a more grounded and pragmatic edge to the Type 9's demeanor. These individuals are often seen as approachable leaders—capable of navigating complex social dynamics with ease, making decisions that prioritize the well-being of the group while ensuring their own needs are not overlooked. The 9w8s are adept at managing conflict, not by avoiding it but by addressing it head-on in a manner that seeks resolution and maintains harmony.

The 9w1: The Peacemaker Joins Forces with the Reformer

On the other side of Type 9 lies the influence of Type 1, the Reformer, resulting in the 9w1 personality. These individuals merge the Type 9's peacekeeping nature with the Type 1's idealistic and principled approach to life. The 9w1s are introspective and often guided by a strong sense of right and wrong, striving to improve themselves and the world around them in quiet, unassuming ways.

The influence of the 1 wing introduces a layer of discipline and order to the Type 9's life, motivating them to engage in practices that align with their values and ideals. The 9w1s are more likely to internalize their quest for peace, focusing on personal integrity and self-improvement as pathways to achieving harmony. While they share the Type 9's aversion to conflict, their approach to dealing with it is more measured and principled, often guided by an internal moral compass.

Navigating the World with Wings

For Type 9 women, understanding the influence of their wings is akin to discovering new dimensions of their personality. It offers insights into their behavior patterns, motivations, and, importantly, their potential for growth. Recognizing the presence of a more assertive 8 wing or a more introspective 1 wing can empower Type 9s to harness these qualities, enabling them to engage more fully with the world and themselves.

In relationships, careers, and personal development, the awareness of their wings allows Type 9s to explore strategies that honor both their core nature and the additional strengths their wings provide. Whether through embracing the 8 wing's courage in advocating for themselves or the 1 wing's commitment to integrity and improvement, Type 9 women can find greater fulfillment and balance.

The exploration of wings within the Enneagram system offers Type 9 women a richer understanding of themselves, revealing the dynamic interplay between their innate peace-seeking nature and the assertive or introspective tendencies of their wings. By embracing the full spectrum of their personality, Type 9s can navigate their journey with greater self-awareness, compassion, and courage, embodying the true essence of the Enneagram's teachings on growth and transformation.

Strengths and Challenges: Embracing the Full Spectrum of Type 9 Wings

For Type 9 women, understanding the interplay between their core personality and their wings (9w8 or 9w1) offers invaluable insights into their unique strengths and challenges. This chapter delves into the gifts and struggles inherent in each wing combination, illuminating the path toward self-discovery and personal growth. Drawing on the Enneagram's ancient roots and its evolution as a guide for self-knowledge, we explore how the distinct characteristics of each wing influence the Type 9's journey, highlighting the ways in which these aspects can be nurtured and balanced.

Type 9w8: The Peacemaker with a Challenger's Edge

Strengths:

Assertiveness: The 9w8 blend combines the Type 9's natural diplomacy with the Type 8's assertiveness, allowing these individuals to stand up for themselves and others with courage and confidence.

Pragmatism: This wing combination equips Type 9s with a practical approach to problem-solving, enabling them to address issues directly and efficiently.

Leadership: The 9w8's unique mix of peacekeeping and decisiveness makes them approachable leaders who can guide with a gentle yet firm hand.

Challenges:

Managing Intensity: The challenge for 9w8s lies in balancing their inner need for peace with the Type 8's intensity, which can sometimes lead to internal conflict between their desire for harmony and their instinct to confront.

Avoiding Burnout: The drive of the 8 wing can push 9w8s to take on more than they can handle, risking burnout as they strive to meet the demands of their environment while maintaining inner calm.

Type 9w1: The Peacemaker with a Reformer's Conscience

Strengths:

Integrity: The 9w1s possess a profound sense of right and wrong, guided by the Type 1's ethical standards, which enriches their peacemaking with principled actions.

Attention to Detail: This wing enhances the Type 9's ability to notice and attend to the finer points in their projects and relationships, allowing for thoroughness and accuracy.

Calm Rationality: 9w1s can approach situations with a calm and rational demeanor, providing a balanced perspective that integrates the Type 9's peace-seeking nature with the Type 1's objective analysis.

Challenges:

Inner Criticism: One of the major challenges for 9w1s is the Type 1's critical inner voice, which can amplify their self-doubt and hinder their natural flow, particularly when their actions do not align with their strict moral standards.

Resistance to Change: The Type 1 wing's penchant for order and routine may reinforce the Type 9's resistance to change, making it difficult for them to step out of their comfort zones.

Balancing Wings and Core Type

For Type 9 women, embracing the strengths of their wings while mitigating the challenges requires self-awareness and active engagement with their personal growth journey. Practices such as mindfulness, self-reflection, and seeking feedback from trusted others can provide insights into how their wings influence their behavior and choices. Moreover, engaging in activities that align with their wing's strengths can further empower Type 9s to express the full breadth of their personality.

The journey of the Type 9 woman is enriched by the nuances of her wings, offering a landscape of potential for growth, leadership, and personal fulfillment. By exploring the strengths and challenges of their wing combinations, Type 9s can navigate their path with greater clarity and purpose. The Enneagram, with its historical depth and transformative power, serves as a compass on this journey, guiding Type 9 women to embrace the complexity of their personalities and to unfold the wings that will carry them towards their true potential.

Chapter 11:

Growth and Transformation: Integration and Disintegration

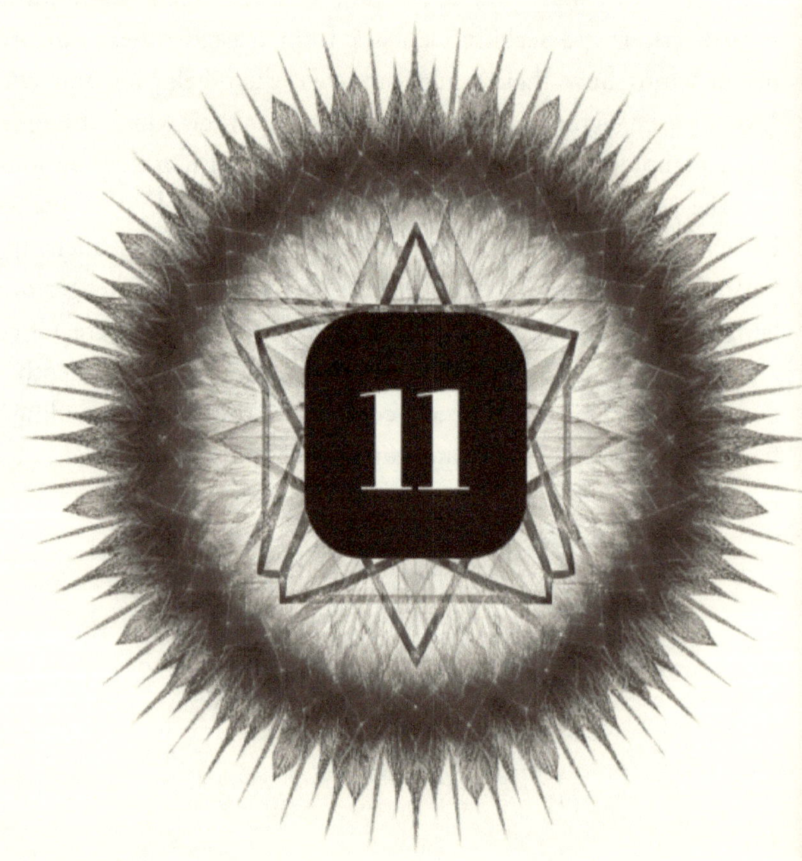

Path of Integration (to Type 3): Activating the Achiever Within

The journey of self-awareness and growth for Type 9 women involves an exploration of paths that lead to both integration and disintegration. Central to the teachings of the Enneagram is the concept that each type has dynamic lines of connection to other types, which manifest in times of growth or stress. For Type 9s, the path of integration leads towards Type 3, the Achiever, signaling a movement towards adopting healthy Type 3 traits such as action, efficiency, and goal orientation. This chapter delves into how Type 9s can embody the positive aspects of Type 3, fostering a transformation that aligns with their quest for personal and professional fulfillment while maintaining their core essence of peace and harmony.

Embracing Action and Efficiency

At their best, Type 3s are characterized by their dynamism, efficiency, and the ability to set and achieve goals. For Type 9s, integrating these traits involves moving from a state of inertia to one of action. It means recognizing the value of their dreams and ambitions and taking deliberate steps towards realizing them. This shift requires Type 9s to engage with their inner drive, setting clear, achievable goals and embracing a more proactive approach to life.

Goal Orientation and the Power of Visualization

Type 9s can further integrate Type 3 characteristics by adopting a goal-oriented mindset. This involves not just setting goals but also visualizing their successful completion. Visualization serves as a powerful motivational tool, helping Type 9s to see beyond immediate obstacles and maintain focus on the end result. By regularly envisioning their achievements, Type 9s can cultivate the determination and confidence typical of Type 3s, driving them to action.

Balancing Ambition with Inner Peace

One of the challenges Type 9s may face on this path of integration is balancing their newfound ambition with their innate desire for peace and harmony. The key lies in pursuing goals that are in harmony with their values and allow for a sense of purpose and fulfillment. Type 9s can achieve this balance by choosing pursuits that resonate with their core identity, ensuring that their actions contribute to a sense of inner satisfaction and peace.

Learning from Failure

Another vital lesson for Type 9s on the path to integration involves embracing failure as a part of the growth process. Type 3s understand that setbacks are not endpoints but stepping stones to greater success. By adopting this perspective, Type 9s can learn to approach failures with resilience, analyzing what went wrong and using these insights to refine their strategies and efforts.

Seeking Feedback and Embracing Visibility

To fully embrace the healthy traits of Type 3, Type 9s are encouraged to seek feedback and embrace visibility. This means stepping out of the shadows and allowing their talents and efforts to be recognized. While this may initially feel uncomfortable, it is a crucial step towards personal growth. Feedback provides valuable insights that can guide Type 9s in their pursuits, while visibility affirms their worth and contributions, bolstering their confidence.

the path of integration towards Type 3 offers a journey of transformation, marked by the adoption of action, efficiency, and a goal-oriented approach. By embracing the strengths of Type 3 while staying true to their essence, Type 9s can unlock new dimensions of their personality, fostering a sense of achievement and fulfillment that coexists with their innate desire for peace and harmony. The Enneagram, with its ancient roots and deep psychological insights, serves as a guide on this journey, offering Type 9s a framework for understanding and embracing the full spectrum of their potential.

Path of Disintegration (to Type 6): Navigating Stress with Awareness

In the intricate journey of self-discovery that Type 9 women embark upon, the Enneagram serves as a map, revealing not only paths to growth but also potential routes to disintegration under stress. For Type 9s, periods of stress and unrest can lead towards characteristics associated with Type 6, the Loyalist, manifesting as increased anxieties, self-doubt, and a heightened sense of insecurity. This chapter explores the dynamics of this transition, offering insights into recognizing these signs and strategies for navigating them, grounded in the ancient wisdom of the Enneagram and its profound insights into human nature.

The Shift to Type 6 Under Stress

Under stress, the typically serene and accommodating Type 9 may find themselves grappling with an inner turmoil that is characteristic of Type 6. This shift can manifest as worry over making the wrong decisions, skepticism about others' intentions, and a pervasive sense of insecurity. The peace-seeking Type 9, in an attempt to avoid conflict and maintain harmony, may inadvertently spiral into cycles of anxiety and indecision, mirroring the Type 6's struggle with trust and fear.

Recognizing the Signs of Disintegration

For Type 9 women, awareness is the first step towards mitigating the effects of stress-induced disintegration. Signs to watch for include:

Increased Worry: A noticeable shift from their usual go-with-the-flow attitude to a state of worry and overthinking about potential outcomes and the loyalty of those around them.

Seeking Assurance: An uncharacteristic need for constant reassurance from others about their decisions and actions, reflecting the Type 6's quest for security.

Avoidance of Action: A deepening of their natural tendency to avoid conflict and confrontation, driven by fear of making mistakes or upsetting the status quo.

Strategies for Navigating Stress

Grounding Techniques: Practices such as deep breathing, meditation, and mindfulness can help Type 9s remain centered and calm, reducing the impact of stress and anxiety.

Reality Checks: When spiraling into worry, Type 9s can benefit from pausing to assess the reality of their fears. Asking themselves whether their concerns are based on facts or hypotheticals can help in distinguishing between genuine issues and stress-induced anxiety.

Seeking Constructive Feedback: Consulting with trusted individuals who can offer objective perspectives can help Type 9s break the cycle of indecision and reassure them of their path.

Embracing Courage: Acknowledging that fear and worry are natural, but not insurmountable, barriers. Type 9s can cultivate courage by taking small, decisive actions, even in the face of uncertainty.

Journaling: Writing about their experiences, worries, and the triggers that exacerbate their stress can offer Type 9s insights into their patterns of behavior and thought, facilitating a more mindful approach to handling stress.

The path of disintegration to Type 6 under stress is a challenging aspect of the Type 9 woman's journey, yet it also holds opportunities for growth and self-awareness. By recognizing the signs of stress-induced anxiety and employing strategies to navigate these waters, Type 9s can maintain their equilibrium and continue to cultivate peace, both within themselves and in their interactions with the world. The teachings of the Enneagram, rooted in centuries of spiritual and philosophical exploration, offer a beacon of light on this journey, guiding Type 9 women towards understanding, resilience, and ultimately, transformation.

The Goal of Growth: Nurturing Wholeness through Integration and Managing Disintegration

The Enneagram, with its rich tapestry of ancient wisdom and profound insights into human nature, serves as a guiding light for Type 9 women on their journey towards growth and transformation. This chapter focuses on the pivotal goal of growth for Type 9s, emphasizing the importance of healthy integration into Type 3 traits for proactive engagement with life and providing strategies to manage the tendencies towards disintegration under stress, which can lead to Type 6 behaviors of anxiety and self-doubt.

The Essence of Integration for Type 9s

Integration for Type 9s involves the conscious cultivation of Type 3's dynamic qualities of action, goal-orientation, and self-confidence. This path of growth encourages Type 9s to move beyond their comfort zones of peace and stability, embracing the challenge of engaging more fully with their ambitions and desires. Healthy integration fosters a sense of agency in Type 9s, enabling them to assert themselves in the pursuit of their goals while maintaining their inherent values of harmony and inclusivity.

Strategies for Healthy Integration

Setting Clear, Achievable Goals: Type 9s can benefit from identifying specific, measurable objectives that align with their passions and values, breaking these down into actionable steps to foster a sense of progress and accomplishment.

Cultivating Self-Discipline: Building routines that encourage productivity and personal accountability can help Type 9s develop the discipline characteristic of healthy Type 3s, balancing their inclination towards inertia with purposeful action.

Embracing Challenges: Viewing challenges as opportunities for growth, rather than threats to peace, allows Type 9s to engage with life more assertively, mirroring the resilience and ambition of Type 3s.

Seeking Feedback: Constructive feedback from trusted peers or mentors can provide Type 9s with valuable insights into their strengths and areas for growth, encouraging a more objective view of their achievements and potential.

Managing the Path of Disintegration

While the journey towards integration represents growth, Type 9s also need strategies to manage the disintegration towards Type 6, especially under stress. Recognizing the signs of anxiety, doubt, and indecision early on can enable Type 9s to implement coping strategies that mitigate these effects and maintain their equilibrium.

Practicing Mindfulness: Mindfulness and meditation can help Type 9s stay grounded in the present moment, reducing the tendency towards worry and speculation characteristic of Type 6 stress patterns.

Strengthening Support Systems: Leaning on a supportive community during times of stress can provide Type 9s with reassurance and perspective, countering feelings of isolation and self-doubt.

Engaging in Physical Activity: Regular physical exercise can serve as an effective outlet for stress, promoting mental clarity and emotional resilience.

Reflecting on Past Successes: Reminding themselves of their past achievements and strengths can help Type 9s counteract the self-doubt and insecurity that arise during disintegration.

the Enneagram offers a comprehensive framework for understanding their unique path towards growth and fulfillment. By embracing the qualities of Type 3 through healthy integration, Type 9s can cultivate a more active and purposeful engagement with life, achieving their goals while remaining true to their core values of peace and harmony. Simultaneously, understanding and managing the tendencies towards disintegration under stress ensures that Type 9s can navigate life's challenges with grace and resilience. Through this balanced approach to growth and transformation, Type 9s can achieve a state of wholeness, where peace is not merely the absence of conflict but the presence of dynamic, fulfilled engagement with the world.

CHAPTER 12:

WORKBOOK

Did you love *The woman of Enneagram 9: Love marriage success edition*?
Then you should read *The woman of Enneagram 8: Love marriage success
edition*[1] by Maria Rondon!

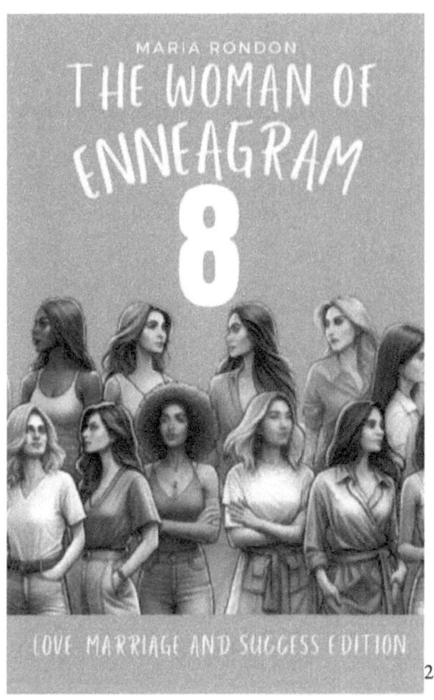

Enneagram Type 8 Woman: Unleashing Your Powerful Authenticity

Discover the transformative power of the Enneagram as a Type 8
woman. This life-changing book provides invaluable insights into the
core motivations, strengths, and growth opportunities for the
Challenger personality type.

As an Enneagram Type 8, you are a powerful, confident, and direct
individual. Your willingness to take charge, confront injustice, and
protect the vulnerable are admirable qualities. However, these traits can
sometimes lead to excessive confrontation, difficulty with vulnerability,
and a tendency to disregard others' perspectives. This book empowers

---

1. https://books2read.com/u/bOpr1W

2. https://books2read.com/u/bOpr1W

you to embrace your true essence while guiding you towards a more balanced and impactful expression of your strengths.

Through thought-provoking exercises and real-life examples, you'll explore how the Enneagram impacts your relationships, career, and personal growth journey. Gain a deeper understanding of your driving needs for control and justice, learn to channel your intensity constructively, and develop emotional intelligence and empathy.

Whether you're seeking to improve your relationships, achieve greater professional success, or simply live a more authentic and fulfilling life, this book is a powerful guide. It offers practical strategies and insights to help you harness the strengths of your Type 8 personality while addressing your core fears and blind spots.

Dive into this life-changing book today and embark on a journey of self-discovery, personal empowerment, and profound growth. Unlock your true potential as an Enneagram Type 8 woman and live with greater presence, purpose, and inner peace, while unleashing the powerful authenticity that makes you a force to be reckoned with.

Also by Maria Rondon

Alzheimer
Alzheimer Guia para cuidadores

Enneagram For Women
The woman of Enneagram 1: Love Marriage Success Edition
The woman of enneagram 2
The woman of Enneagram 3: Love marriage success edition
The Woman of Enneagram 4: Love, Marriage, Success Edition
The woman of Enneagram 5: Love marriage success edition
The Woman of Enneagram 6: Love, Marriage, Success Edition
The woman of Enneagram 7: Love marriage success edition
The woman of Enneagram 8: Love marriage success edition
The woman of Enneagram 9: Love marriage success edition

LOA
El secreto para atraer tu alma gemela

Standalone

Keto Low-Carb Mexican Cookbook
Plant Powered Cookbook: The Ultimate Vegan Cookbook for Healthy Living
The Destiny Matrix